SELF-TREATMENT FOR COLITIS

Twenty million pounds a year are spent on drugs which fail to cure the various forms of colitis, or inflammation of the large bowel. Harry Clements describes how the condition may be cured by treating the whole system through natural foods and relaxation techniques.

By the same author
DIETS TO HELP KIDNEY DISORDERS
DIETS TO HELP PROSTATE TROUBLES
DIETS TO HELP PSORIASIS

In this series
ARTHRITIS — THE CONQUEST!
BANISHING BACKACHE AND DISC TROUBLES
HEADACHES AND MIGRAINE
NATURE CURE FOR CONSTIPATION
NATURE CURE FOR PAINFUL JOINTS
NATURE CURE FOR PROSTATE TROUBLES
NATURE CURE FOR SHINGLES AND COLD SORES
SELF-TREATMENT FOR HERNIA
SELF-TREATMENT FOR SKIN TROUBLES

Self-Treatment for Colitis

Harry Clements N.D., D.O.

THORSONS PUBLISHERS LIMITED
Wellingborough, Northamptonshire

First published 1978
Second Impression 1980
Third Impression 1982
Fourth Impression 1984
Fifth Impression 1986

© HARRY CLEMENTS 1978

This book is sold subject to the condition that it shall not, by way of trade or otherwise, be lent, re-sold, hired out, or otherwise circulated without the publisher's prior consent in any form of binding or cover other than that in which it is published and without a similar condition including this condition being imposed on the subsequent purchaser.

ISBN 0 7225 0452 7

Printed and bound in Great Britain by
Richard Clay (The Chaucer Press) Ltd.,
Bungay, Suffolk.

Contents

	Page
Foreword	7
Chapter	
1. What is Colitis?	9
2. Understanding Colitis	12
3. Colitis and 'Nerves'	19
4. What Causes Colitis?	26
5. Understanding the Symptoms	35
6. Self-Help Treatment for Colitis	42

Foreword

Colitis is an illness of which it might rightly be said that self-help and self-care, can and do play a very important part in its treatment. It is a complaint for which there is no known specific remedy, so that those who suffer from it must rely on efforts which he or she must make for themselves. In this complaint, in which constipation is such a contributing factor, it is clearly necessary that much attention must be paid to those things which will prevent it or overcome it when it exists. This means that diet must play a significant part in any form of treatment, and diet to be of real effectiveness must demand the intelligent cooperation of the patient. It is not something that may be done for him by proxy. It must become a part of his life-style and clearly no one can live life for another person. The same is true of rest, sleep and relaxation and other habits which enter into the life-style of all of us. These habits, when sensibly observed, make all the difference between health and illness, for if neglect or indifference to these things lead to depletion of the vital energy of the body the likelihood of illness occuring, is of course, multiplied. When a person is enervated in this way the metabolism of the system is upset, and the waste products of its activity retained in the tissues and organs leading to auto-intoxication, ill health and the particular disease reaction to which the individual may be predisposed.

In the circumstances, it should be apparent that self-help and self-care is of paramount importance, and that nature cure is fundamental to all methods of healing. In order that people should practise self-help and self-care it may be necessary for them to relearn many things which have been overlooked through the present obsession with medicines. In this respect, perhaps we should remind ourselves that the word doctor means teacher, and that is something else that might be readopted at the present time with great advantage and benefit to the individual and to the community. It can justly be claimed that only Nature Cure remains steadfast to the idea that freedom from ill-health and disease will come, not through medicines or some other scientific discovery, but through the removal of the causes of disease and through the adoption of a way of life that is in according with the laws of nature.

1.
What is Colitis?

Colitis simply means an inflammation of the colon or large bowel, but the term may be very misleading it gives the impression that it is a local condition confined to the organ involved. The same misunderstanding has occurred in other such cases, particularly with arthritis which simply means an inflammation of a joint. At first, it gave the impression of its being of purely local origin, but we now know that it is in fact a constitutional disease. It is important to make this distinction quite clear because obviously the kind of treatment will depend on such an interpretation. If colitis were just a local condition then it might make sense to treat it by local measures; if on the other hand, it does involve the whole body and personality of the individual it is perfectly clear that nothing less than taking the whole person and his environment into consideration will provide us with the knowledge on which successful treatment will be based.

TREATING THE WHOLE BODY

Consideration of this viewpoint in relation to colitis brings us into the controversy between the Nature Cure interpretation of such illness and that of the orthodox profession. This brings us, of course, to the idea of the unitary concept in health and disease in which we assume that anything being strictly local must be a misconception. To sustain such a concept seems to be so simple. No part or organ of the body exists for or by itself. It has to be supplied by the nerves and the blood and other fluids and it has to take part in the general breaking down and building up processes that are constantly going on. Every cell in the body has to be supplied with essential nutriments and the waste products which every cell produces have to be carried away. How then can one argue that any condition of health or disease can be entirely local and in asking ourselves the question: 'what is colitis?' we must look for the answer in a far wider field than a merely local one.

FORMS OF COLITIS

Colitis is a widespread complaint affecting people of all ages and both sexes, although figures seem to show that women are rather more prone to it. It is a disease of varied degrees; it can be of a mild character and, in its early days, may be neglected. But it can lead to very serious conditions that break down the resistance of the tissues, leading to ulceration and haemorrhages. Its main feature, apart from abdominal pain and distress and flatulence, is the passage with the stools of mucus in larger or lesser amounts depending, of course on the severity or otherwise of the trouble. Colitis, then, is a disorder of the colon or large bowel, and as the function of this organ is largely the elimination of waste products from the digestive tract, it is peculiarly vulnerable to irritation, particularly if there is sluggishness in waste removal.

It would be wrong to assume that all the symptoms in colitis relate only to the bowel and the abdominal region. There are usually many other symptoms of ill health present at the same time. Among them we may list headaches, flatulence and stomach acidity, bad taste in the mouth and possibly bad breath, nausea and other disturbances of the digestive system. And, with these symptoms, there are often ones affecting the nervous system which has led people to think that a nervous temperament is more to blame for the complaint than the physical counterpart. In many cases so much credence has been given to this view that other important aspects of the illness have been overlooked. That it is 'mostly in the mind' is an attitude in any kind of illness that can leave the patient and practitioner in a pretty hopeless position. Of course the mind can play a very important part in the complaint and in its treatment, but in such cases it is always wrong to try to separate the body and the mind and to consider one to be more important that the other. In life they exist together in unity and they do so in all forms of ill-health.

COLITIS AND THE WAY WE LIVE

If we think of colitis as an illness involving both the body and the mind, and not merely as an inflammation of one part of the body, then the idea of treating it with specific remedies becomes somewhat of an absurdity. Coexisting with the symptoms of colitis, as we have pointed out, are many other symptoms as well and if we were trying to suppress them with medicines we should have to be using many different ones at the same time: one for the headaches, one for the flatulence and another for the nausea and so on. Apart from the complications of so doing, there would be the difficulty of the various drugs reacting with each other and possibly cancelling out the desired effect.

On the other hand if it is possible to show that colitis is the result of certain conditions involving the way of living and the daily habits which have, step by step, undermined the health and resistance of the body and thus caused the illness, then it seems to be only commonsense that such conditions should be investigated, removed, modified or corrected as far as possible, so that the fullness of bodily and nervous health can be regained. Mistaken habits of living, stress and strains of all kinds deplete the stock of nervous energy, and, in consequence, normal functions of the body become disordered and complaints like colitis develop since it is no exception to this rule.

2.
Understanding Colitis

Understanding the nature of an illness can be very helpful in its proper management and certainly this is true of colitis, and as it is closely related to the digestive processes and the utilization of food a short description of the alimentary canal and its function may be in place. The sufferer from almost any kind of illness has some kind of responsibility for its treatment although it is true that the development of modern medicine, with its powerful drugs, have tended to minimize the part which the individual plays in this way — a fact which some authorities, Ivan Illich among them, see as a retrograde step. Certainly from the Nature Cure viewpoint it is to be very much deplored.

THE ALIMENTARY CANAL
In a sense the alimentary canal is outside the body tissues since it runs right through the body. It is a long muscular tube beginning at the mouth and terminating at the rectum. The canal is designed to hold a large amount of food which it has to digest and prepare for absorption into the body, and it has also to dispose of the parts of the food which are not digestible. The stomach is the container of food, the part of the alimentary canal known as the small intestine is concerned with the absorption of it while the colon or large bowel has to deal with the absorption of water and the elimination of the

waste products of digestion. The mouth acts as a mill grinding up the food and mixing it with the saliva so that it becomes a form of paste before being passed on to the stomach. The thorough chewing of the food is important, not only because it makes its digestion easier for the stomach but because it also alerts the stomach to the fact that food is on the way. The stomach carries on with the digestive process, churning up the food and mixing it with the digestive juices and then passing it on to the small intestine for absorption into the blood. After this has been accomplished the remainder of the food residue enters into the large bowel for elimination from the system.

THE DIGESTIVE SYSTEM IN ACTION

This is, of course, a gross simplification of a process that borders on the miraculous and which still has within itself chemical and other problems that have not been fully resolved; but this bare outline of it should be kept in mind when disordered functions of the digestive system, as may happen in colitis, are being discussed. Let us now try to visualize what happens in the digestive system when the three meals of the day are taken. Breakfast may be taken at about 8.30 a.m. and it may be an ordinary meal consisting perhaps of fruit and some form of cereal. Previous to this may have been a cup of tea. If the digestion is in a normal state and we could follow the passage of the food, by the time the midday meal is taken, at say 1 o'clock, the remains of the breakfast would have reached the small intestine and be undergoing absorption into the blood, with the fore part of it just entering the colon. Then at about 6 p.m. when the evening meal is taken, all of the breakfast meal will have been digested and absorbed and the remainder of it will now be about half way through the colon, with most of the midday meal residue in the other half. If more food were taken in the evening it would then be following the residue of the midday meal which would have reached the lower part of the bowel and be ready for evacuation.

All these movements of the food and its residue through the alimentary canal can greatly vary in individual cases, but a simple outline is given here to give the reader an idea of what happens in the passage of food and its utilization in the canal when the functions are relatively normal. It is, of course the conception of the digestive system working under ideal circumstances with foods ideally suited for its purposes, but, unfortunately, such conditions are the exception rather than the rule. It may appear, perhaps, as though the whole process is entirely automatic but as a matter of fact it uses up a great deal of nervous and muscular energy and it is easy to imagine how many things may dissipate such energy. Indigestible food, overeating, hurried eating and eating under stress, may add to the burden of the digestive process and be a drain on the vital energy, thus upsetting the rhythm of the whole system. People often forget such things so far as digestion is concerned. For instance, they may eat between meals and thus add to the difficulties of it and many other habits such as excessive drinking and smoking can very definitely have an adverse effect upon the stomach and other parts of the alimentary canal and one should always bear in mind that no one part of the digestive system can be adversely affected without, in some measure, affecting the whole of it.

CAUSES OF DIGESTIVE DISORDERS

When the stomach is upset, which may happen from many causes, it will not be able to deal properly with the preparation of the food, and, in consequence, this will interfere with the absorption of it into the blood that takes place in the small intestine. This will affect the nutrition of the body and the general health will suffer. And there may be a further adverse effect in that the residue of the food entering the colon for elimination may not have been suitably prepared for the purpose. Again, if the food taken into the body is of an over-refined and over-concentrated sort, commonly in use today, there may be a lack of roughage or indigestible substances in the food waste to stimulate the large bowel into action. As a result it will move more slowly through the passage of the bowel, tending to distend it and be retained in its lower part. And this condition constitutes the first stage in the development of constipation.

By far the majority of people who find themselves in this condition will start the laxative habit and they may be fairly sure that unless they change their dietary habits the former will be with them for most part of their lives, with the strong possibility that the side effects of the laxative drugs take the form of diverticula (pouch formations in the walls of the bowels), haemorrhoids, and, in susceptible cases, colitis. These people will join with all the others who at the present time are said to be spending well over twenty million pounds yearly on laxative drugs.

LAXATIVES

It is worthwhile considering for a moment what a laxative is and what occurs when it is taken into the body. It may be of mineral or vegetable origin. Liquid paraffin, a mineral oil was at one time considered to be an ideal laxative lubricant. It was heralded with as much enthusiasm as bran is today, and it had many advocates including Sir Arbuthnot Lane, the famous surgeon, among others. However like so many other medical remedies whose virtues have been so loudly proclaimed, time and the appearance of side effects put a stop to the mineral oil craze. It became evident that in acting as a lubricant it interfered with the natural lubrication of the body, and even more importantly it interfered with the synthesis of vitamin D which takes place in the large colon. But the last straw was the discovery that it was found to be associated with the cause of cancer, and this naturally deterred doctors and patients from making use of it. So that now it is used only in exceptional cases or by those who have no real knowledge of its possible dangers. Epsom salts and other mineral salts are also used in this respect and they act by drawing the fluids into the bowel and producing liquid stools that are more freely evacuated.

But, in the main, the vegetable kingdom is the chief source of the laxatives and purgatives. The difference between them is more a matter of degree rather than of kind. A purgative, of which there are a great many, including such well known ones as castor oil, aloes, jalap and so on, cause a drastic action in the bowel whereas a laxative has a much milder effect. While the purgative may be used where a more drastic evacuation is desired, it is the milder laxative that is used in the majority of cases and which becomes habit-forming. In any case, these laxatives act mainly through irritation which induces the body to make the effort to expel them and thus remove the accumulated wastes as well. Some people are under the false impression that if a remedy is of vegetable or herbal origin it is free from harmful effects, but this is by no means true. The purgatives mentioned above are of that origin and yet they are capable of causing the most violent reactions in the bowel.

No laxative of any kind is entirely free of side effects and habitual irritation of the bowel by their use will cause congestion in the tissues leading to catarrhal secretions and other changes especially like haemorrhoids. But the most logical objection to them is the fact that they allow their users to continue with the same kind of diet that is at the source of their bowel complaints. That this is so has been clearly shown recently by the fact that if the roughage or fibre of food, such as bran, is retained in the diet the bowel action will be normally carried out. But, here again, people are inclined to act foolishly. Instead of using wholewheat bread which contains the bran in proper quantity and balance, and preparing the vegetables and fruit so that their fibrous parts are not lost, they maintain all the old habits of refined foods, white flour, white sugar and so on, and then dose themselves with bran possibly in excessive quantities, and they feel disappointed if things go wrong.

LONG-TERM EFFECTS OF LAXATIVES
Constipation, and the use of laxatives, if continued over a period of time will bring about changes in the mucous membranes and the walls of the bowel. They may become slightly congested and

inflamed with attacks of diarrhoea in the early stages of the trouble. This may indeed be the first sign that unless prompt and effective measures are taken to restore the integrity of the bowel the condition may lead to an attack of colitis. At this time there is the real danger also that if the resistance of the bowel becomes weakened an infective process may develop which means, of course, that a further dimension has been added to the problem: bacterial activity. At this stage the illness will be in its acute form with all the typical symptoms and with the discharge of mucus with the stools.

The complaint is a progressive one and unless checked by suitable and effective treatment can develop into the chronic form in which abdominal discomfort will be accompanied by bouts of severe pains and the passing of the mucous stools. Again, if the trouble progresses still further a breakdown in the tissues may occur with the possibility of ulceration, and in very severe occasions haemorrhages. Naturally it follows that if this stage has been reached the general health of the individual will cause great concern, but if the case had been recognized in the early stages and properly managed such a severe and serious situation should not have arisen.

Not all cases of constipation and users of laxatives for its treatment will develop into colitis, of course, and this may be explained by the fact that each person probably has within himself the seeds of the illnesses to which he may be constitutionally predisposed. Before the development and use of the modern powerful drugs, which are used without any attention being paid to the individuality of the patient or to the variety of people, much more interest was paid to these facts. Doctors and others used the term diathesis in the management of patients, implying, of course, that the patient had a predisposition to a certain form of disease and this was taken into consideration when planning treatment. It was helpful, too, in preventive medicine since it gave the adviser some idea of what might happen in the future and how it might be avoided by altering the way of life and the daily habits which contribute to the future breakdown in health.

It also helped the individual to take more interest in the subject of healthy living and the prevention of illness, and to understand the various changes that take place in the early stages of it so that steps might be taken to alter course before it is too late. In colitis, such an understanding is very important for the simple reason that it is much easier to deal with it in the earlier days than when it has run on to the chronic stage. This is true, of course, of most chronic illnesses: they become chronic only after long periods of time when they are neglected or when the treatment has been ineffective. It is therefore of real importance in an illness like colitis for the sufferer to make an effort to understand what has happened in his body and the way in which his illness has developed. It will help him to discover causative factors, to take an intelligent interest in the treatment and will be a real help in resolving his problems.

3.
Colitis and 'Nerves'

One of the notions about colitis that, to a certain extent, bedevilled the rational physical treatment of it has been the belief that the cause of it is largely of nervous origin and therefore very difficult to overcome. It seems to follow that, if it is accepted that it is 'mostly in the mind', the sufferer is then regarded as one almost more to be pitied than to be treated, since the latter is likely to meet with very little success. Such an attitude can be unhelpful in any kind of illness; in colitis it is simply disastrous, for no complaint is more likely to undermine a sufferer's confidence that this particular one, and confidence is an essential ingredient in all forms of treatment as it is in all other forms of life.

In this respect it is interesting to look back at the medical attitude toward the complaint at the beginning of this century when one of the great medical teachers who was regarded as an authority on such matters wrote in his textbook: 'In a large proportion of all the cases the subjects are nervous in greater or less degree. Some cases have had hysterical outbreaks, and there may be hypochondriasis or melancholia. The patients are self-centred and often much worried about the mucous stools. Some of the cases are the most distressing with which we have to deal, invalids of from ten to twenty years standing, neurasthenic to an extreme degree, with recurring attacks of pain and the passage of large quantitites of mucus in the stool.'

The emphasis here was clearly on the neurasthenic state of the patient which meant that nervous debility was at the back of the trouble which made the complaint one that was very difficult to treat successfully, since, as we know, when the trouble is said to be of nervous origin it usually implies that ordinary physical methods are not of much use. The same authority enlarging on the nature of the complaint said that it had been known and discussed for centuries, and at the time of his writing he declared that it 'had greatly increased, and was becoming a fashionable complaint.' This attitude has prevailed over the years and there is no doubt that it had had a powerful influence on the complaint and on the patient and his advisers.

When reading Dr Osler's description of the sufferer from the complaint one can easily imagine that anyone suffering from the physical discomforts of it might very readily show all the nervous disorders which he mentions. How could the person feel other than worried and at times be so frustrated as to become hysterical and melancholic, especially since so little help was forthcoming as the doctor's attitude clearly admitted. What was worse, of course, was the effect on the patient who seemed to be told that it was mostly a matter of 'pulling himself together'. Labelling a patient as neurotic, especially if he was suffering all the physical discomforts of an illness like colitis, was about the worse insult that could be offered to him.

NUTRITION AND NERVOUS DISORDERS

Fortunately, in more recent times there has been a great change in the attitude of many authorities about the nature of mental and nervous disorders. It is now seen that bodily dysfunction, due particularly to nutritional deficiency and other physical disturbances, can be causative factors and this, of course, has given fresh hope to sufferers. When we look at this from the viewpoint of commonsense we see how reasonable these ideas are. Nutrition is fundamental to all forms of mental, emotional and physical activity and a disturbed digestive system such as may be found in complaints like colitis is certain to lead to nutritional deficiencies. It is a well established fact that in deficiency diseases there may be very serious mental and nervous disorders, and an illness that drains the system of its vital energy will make it unable to make proper use of its food, and consequently its nutritional state will be at risk. The brain cells depend upon sound nutrition just as much as any other cells in the body and without it they cannot operate efficiently with the possible result that nervous disorders will occur. It is wrong to think that depression, neurasthenia, hysteria, melancholia and so on, have no relation to the physical condition of the body and are not the expression of disordered nutrition. It is probably because people have not properly related the physical and mental to each other that real solutions to many complaints have not been forthcoming. The simple fact is that what we eat, and the way in which it is digested and utilized in the body is just as much the basis of sound mental and nervous health as it is of physical well-being.

When we talk of a deficiency diet and its possibility of undermining the nutrition and causing nervous disorders, we should remember that a deficiency may occur, not only from food lacking in quantity and quality, but also from the inability of the body to digest and absorb it. This may often happen in illness like colitis, and as a result of it nutrition will be very poor, the body will lose weight, a typical symptom of the chronic state. And, again we must bear in mind that in such a condition the brain cells will share in the starvation just as much as any other part of the body. It is only reasonable to suggest that unless the brain cells receive proper and adequate nutrients they cannot function efficiently, and the fact is, of course, that they can only get such nutrients *from the food we eat*. Without such nutrients we must expect that the whole nervous system will suffer in some way or other and the personality of the individual will undergo changes which may be designated as depression, neuroticism, melancholia, hysteria and so on.

The reader may feel perhaps, that we have over-emphasized the importance of food in the prevention and management of colitis to the exclusion of other ways of helping the sufferer akin to psychology, relaxation and such other therapeutic measures. But this is by no means so. The over-emphasis on food and nutrition, if that is what it is, has been done to a large extent to counteract the common attitude that the nervous symptoms are all-important and should be given priority in treatment. This has led to the fact that many of the sufferers are left without proper guidance about their food and its selection to suit their own case. If one looks through the many books and publications on psychiatry and psychotherapy one will find very little reference to the importance of diet. From the Nature Cure viewpoint the one fact which is basic to all its ideas about health and disease is the importance of good, and as nearly as possible, natural food. On this matter it agrees wholeheartedly with the axiom laid down by the famous nutritionist Sir Robert McCarrison who wrote: 'It may, therefore, be taken as a law of life, infringement of which will surely bring its own penalties, that the greatest single factor in the acquisition and maintainance of good health is properly constituted food.' We would carry this thought still further and suggest that good natural food should be given priority in the treatment of all forms of illness no matter what other method of treatment is being used and it is a matter of regret that the use of modern drugs have tended to obscure the importance of this essential requirement.

In all forms of illness, and, of course, colitis is no exception, the personality of the patient counts for a great deal and must always be taken into consideration. People do differ enormously in any circumstance, and it is likely that a complaint like colitis, which can be so trying in so many respects, would undermine a person's morale and thus portray a weak and dependent character. In such a state the sufferer would be far more liable to give way under any form of stress, mental, emotional or physical and this in turn would have an adverse effect upon the illness. The explanation here may be that this type of personality is inclined to bottle up his feelings too much and produce within himself a conflict that would keep him tense and use up a great deal of nervous energy. Of course, these generalizations are true of many people, whether they are colitis sufferers or not; but there is no doubt that such inner conflicts do most markedly exacerbate the colitis symptoms.

THE EFFECT OF STRESS
Living as people do in stressful circumstances these situations cannot always be avoided but it is possible by a little self-analysis one can in some measure make oneself more immune to such circumstances which is well worthwhile. People, when they are ill, tend to lose confidence in themselves and to become more dependent on others. To help them to restore such confidence by reassurance is most helpful in colitis, and if a patient is going through a crisis due to some emotional or other strain its temporary nature should be emphasized – a fact that the person can well tell himself!

While we would contend that mental, emotional and other stressful conditions are not the basic cause of colitis, we would be equally willing to agree that once such conflicts are in existence they most certainly place an important part in exacerbating and maintaining the trouble. We know, for instance, that many people when under mental strain, as from stage fright, may suffer from looseness of the bowel which is a clear indication of the reflex connection between it and the mental processes. This hyperactivity of the walls of the colon, while it may be only temporary with healthy people, quite obviously would have much more effect on those who are suffering from colitis. In the face of these bouts of nervous tension the patient must learn to protect himself by conscious relaxation. It is the answer to modern nervous tension, which is as prevalent in industrial societies, and is far safer than the use of drug tranquillizers and anti-depressants, all of which are certain to produce side effects.

RELAXATION
Relaxing the body and mind in this way may sound very easy but

actually it is a very difficult thing to do, especially for those who are temperamentally and muscularly tense, as sufferers from digestive and bowel troubles generally are. But it is simply indispensable if the troubles are to be successfully overcome. It is so important for colitis sufferers that they should set aside a period of the day, half an hour or so, and practise assiduously conscious relaxation. And it should also be done at evening time just before going to sleep which, incidentally, it will make much more restful and refreshing. Such relaxation naturally calls for the exercise of considerable will power and this in itself can make an important contribution to self-healing.

RELAXATION TECHNIQUES

A great many techniques have been developed covering the art of conscious relaxation, but the simple fact is that unless the performer is a willing cooperator they amount to very little. The fact is that it is very much a do-it-yourself performance, and although one may be told to relax the arms and legs by 'letting them go' it is only by patience and persistence that will make the relaxation a reality. There have been many books published on the subject and our experience has been that their usefulness is in ratio with the reader's desire and will to make use of them. Experience has shown that the following plan works very well for many people:

The subject must be in a room that is warm, free as far as possible of noise and glaring lights. The best position for most people is lying on the back with a small cushion under the neck and with other thick cushions propping the knees up so as to take the strain off the lower back. The breathing should be gentle and rhythmic and all the muscles of the body, the legs and the arms are allowed to relax as much as possible.

Many people find it very difficult when relaxing the body in this way to relax the mind as well and unless this is done the relaxation will not be complete. A great help in this respect is to make a special attempt to relax the eyes. One should remember that those of us who live and work in cities keep the eyes under a great deal of strain.

Apart from living under artificial light much of the time, in many occupations the eyes are constantly used in close work which often bring them to the point of fatigue. The use of spectacles, too, may tend to stretch the eyes beyond their natural capacity and tire them. It is, therefore, imperative to relax the eyes so as to help in the relaxation of the mind and the body and the following method has been found to be an efficacious way of doing so:

While still lying on the back in the relaxed condition close the eyes and cover them with the palms of the hands. In many cases, when the eyes are tired and strained from overwork, the performer will not visualize black as he should normally do, but still see signs of light. An effort of the imagination should be made to blacken them out so that the eyes are set at rest. If this is done successfully it will help to put the mind at rest and assist in the relaxation of the whole body. This relaxing exercise can be extended still further by using the imagination in trying to visualize pleasant memories and scenes. With the eyes still closed and covered by the palms of the hands try to think of some very pleasant happening in past life, such as a part of a memorable holiday that was pleasant, and if you have a visualize memory endeavour to go over the scenes relating to it. This will make the period of relaxation very interesting and pleasurable, and go far in producing a relaxed state of mind and body. Incidentally, many will find that the eyes will benefit also since there is no doubt that nervous tension of the mind and body does affect the sight and other senses also, all of which will benefit by conscious relaxation.

Colitis sufferers who have been told that 'nerves' are a major factor in their troubles should make special effort to practice conscious relaxation. If they are afflicted with depression and other such nervous reactions they will find it most helpful, and at the same time they may be assured that it will be of real assistance in the effective treatment of the bowel dysfunction. Even when the complaint has developed into the more serious condition of ulceration it can be of real help and well worth the time and effort spent on it.

4.
What Causes Colitis?

We are told that, from the medical viewpoint, very little is known about the causative factors in colitis. It is a widespread disease, and it may be found in many industrial countries, differing in numbers but well enough known to be classified as a disease. In most countries where it has been investigated, it relates mainly to ulcerative colitis, and as far as causative factors are concerned, it is generally agreed by the orthodox profession that no specific cause has been found in spite of the fact that it has been known for centuries, and has been subjected to the most thorough and extensive studies. It seems from medical publications on the complaint that it becomes of interest to the profession only when it has developed into the ulcerative state, and one may assume that in the earlier stages of the illness patients only occasionally treated it seriously enough to seek advice and received treatment which was merely palliative and not curative in the real sense of the term.

When the illness has reached the ulcerative stage and causative factors are being considered they are sometimes listed, by the orthodox profession, along the following hypothetical lines: infection, allergy, with milk as the possible allergen, and psychological factors, particularly emotional conflicts. The investigations have been made with the idea of finding a specific cause which might then make it possible for some agent to be found that might lead to successful treatment. Until that happens, which many feel to be doubtful, the medical treatment will have to be of a palliative nature for the relief of symptoms, with surgery as the last choice if that fails.

THE REAL CAUSES

But if on the other hand, we look for causative factors from the Nature Cure viewpoint we adopt a very different attitude. From this viewpoint the ulcerative state of the illness has been reached after a period of time when the body has been subjected to stresses and strains and mistaken habits of living, which have taken their toll of its energy, resistance and reserves. The view is taken that it is a digestive trouble, which, although its manifestation is in the colon, is nevertheless related to the whole function of digestion, absorption and elimination of waste. For, after all, colitis is closely associated with the elimination of the waste products of food that has passed through the alimentary tract and it is in this respect that causative factors should be considered. It can be said, without fear of contradiction, that colitis, both in its simple and in its most serious form, is always associated with constipation, and it is here that we should look for some of the reasons why it is so. The fact that 20 million pounds are spent every year in this country on laxatives is an indication of the extent of this complaint, and this is probably a conservative estimate. What this means is that constipation is a universal complaint.

The basic cause of constipation is easily understood: when the bowel is acting normally the individual becomes aware of its happening through reflex action – the call of Nature – which if responded to quickly, as it should be, ends with the evacuation of the waste products of digestion, together with other toxic substances which are eliminated in the same way. There are no set times for the movement of the bowel, each individual in this respect may be a law unto himself. But, generally speaking, since the retention of the waste products serve no useful purpose, its regular removal at not too long intervals seems to be the best order of things.

Most are aware, of course, of the need for the waste products to be evacuated without undue delay, and when it does not happen, within what appears to be a reasonable time, resort may be had to the use of a laxative medicine of which there are many available on the market. When it is used it stimulates the bowel into action and evacuation takes place. As a rule nothing is done about the basic cause of the constipation: the use of refined and over-concentrated foods and the lack in them of the roughage or natural fibre. So it becomes necessary to rely on laxatives and if these are used over a period of time the laxative habit will have been well established.

The effect on the bowel is predictable in cases where a person is predisposed to colitis, diverticulitis, haemorrhoids and so. As we know the waste products have to be moved by peristaltic action, that is, a muscular action that propels the wastes through the colon so that when it reaches the rectum, the lower end of the bowel, the nervous reflex is set in motion and the contents removed. But when the diet consists mainly of refined foods, and there is an absence of 'roughage' the passage is considerably slowed down and adverse effects on the walls and mucous membranes of the bowel may take place. The waste may also tend to harden and to damage the tissues as it passes along, which in the course of time may lead to congestion and inflammation. In this way constipation may develop and will set the pattern for other illnesses to follow, particulary colitis.

When this condition has persisted for some time changes will take place that will make the person aware of the lack of proper bowel movement. This may be followed by flatulence and abdominal discomfort and sometimes the stomach will share in the discomfort with bouts of indigestion. It may also upset the function of absorption so that this may lead to poor nutrition and signs of ill health. It is not unusual to find such people liable to catarrhal affections which may affect in some degree the whole of the alimentary canal. Disorders of this kind are more likely to happen as a result of constipation rather than from the reabsorption of toxic waste from the large intestine. Once the catarrhal condition has developed, unless effective measures are taken for its treatment, it will very soon turn into its chronic form and all the main mucous membranes of the body may be affected. Such sufferers are very liable to have very heavy colds, to have nausea from stomach catarrh, and there is no doubt that the large intestine will also be affected in a similar way with constipation as the basic cause.

When the bowel has been irritated and distended by the storing up of the residue of the waste products, and with perhaps some minor congestion of the walls and mucous membranes, the body may react occasionally with an attack of diarrhoea in which the waste products will be liquidized and removed drastically. Such a reaction of the body is initiated in its own interest and for a beneficial purpose in the circumstances, but, here again, the mistake may be made of trying to suppress it with powerful drugs which may well lead on to further trouble. In any case a period has now been entered when the patient is liable to suffer from alternate bouts of constipation and diarrhoea, and this often signifies the starting point of simple colitis.

When this condition does develop, mainly through the use of refined, denatured foods like white bread, white flour and the many other products made with it, white sugar and the numerous foods in which this 'pure, white and deadly' substance has been used, and all the other over-prepared, packaged and convenience foods, the patient may then have been told to live on a bland diet in which there is very little residue of fibre, the very thing which has contributed to the making of his complaint. In this condition, where there may be looseness of the bowel and occasional attacks of diarrhoea, the idea of avoiding any food that might add to the irritation, rather naturally appeals to the patient; but the fact is that unless the bowel can be restored to a condition where more natural foods can be taken there will be very little hope of recovery.

THE PRICE OF CONVENIENCE FOODS

Another interesting point in this connection is that people who live on these refined, denatured foods are also the consumers of generous amounts of meat and other animal products and these foods are particularly harmful where there is constipation. It should be remembered that fruits and vegetables tend to ferment in the body, whereas the animal products may putrify, and as we know when food poisoning takes place, it is the protein foods that are chiefly to blame. It is also, of course, a fact that these foods are more liable to produce toxic waste products so that when a person is suffering from constipation the retention of these wastes may be more liable to have an adverse effect on the mucous membranes of the bowel and may be a contributing factor in the colitis. People who eat meat should remember that the use of fruit and vegetables is an antidote and should be very regularly and freely used for that purpose.

ALLERGIC REACTIONS

When we are considering the part played by food in causing colitis we must, of course, take into consideration the part which some foods may have as allergens, that is, as agents which cause allergic reactions. The one food which has come under suspicion in this respect is milk, and while the medical authorities are not entirely convinced that it should be proscribed in colitis, in practice one will find that most doctors will warn patients against its use. Whether in itself, it may cause colitis seems unlikely but there is no doubt that when colitis has developed milk should not be used in planning a suitable diet. There are plenty of other foods to choose from and its omission is not a serious loss. If milk is used at all it should not be used with refined foods; if its use for some reason is very much desired it should always be combined with acid fruit or fruit juices which will help in curdling it and thus make its digestion much easier. Milk taken in bulk and added to a full meal containing other animal products, plus sugar and other carbohydrate foods, is simply asking for indigestion and other troubles and would certainly be out of the question for anyone suffering from colitis.

The medical profession seem to pay very little attention to diet in the treatment of many forms of illness and this is especially true of colitis. Apart from the idea that milk may be a causative factor in it, it seems that not much attention is paid otherwise to the possible influence of food. A quote from a medical book published in 1977 emphasizes the point: 'There is no evidence that dietary factors play any part in the cause of ulcerative colitis apart from a small percentage of patients who benefit from the exclusion of milk and milk containing items ...'

The same writer, however, in almost the same paragraph, says that 'constipation is so often a major feature in ulcerative colitis.' But surely if constipation is such a major feature in the illness then it seems obvious that the same factor which causes it, a lack of fibre in the food, must also be of importance in the treatment of colitis. It is difficult to see how two forms of illness can be separated in this way.

DIAGNOSING ALLERGIES

When an allergy deriving from some particular food is under suspicion efforts should be made to discover just what it is. Many different methods have been used for this purpose including injections and the pulse tests, in which variations in the beating of the pulse are noted after each meal. This method had its advocates in America, but it seems to have met with less enthusiasm elsewhere.

Another method that can be used by the individual, and is a valuable way of determining if a particular food may not be suitable, is known as the mono-diet in which a single factor of food is used at a meal and its effects carefully noted. If there is no reaction on the complaint, as for example on the colitis, another food is added to the meals and noted in the same manner. In this way the whole diet is built up with a very good chance of its being the most suitable one. If, of course, any particular food does cause a reaction its use is most carefully avoided. It is quite well known that some people do react to certain foods: strawberries are a good general example, and anyone who has had experience in dieting patients will know that other foods can have a similar effect on some people. These may take the form of skin eruptions and in the writer's own experience a Scots woman suffered an extensive skin rash after taking oat porridge! Food allergy should always be considered especially in an illness like colitis where there is obviously hypersensitivity in the mucous membranes of the digestive organs, and when the offending food or substance can be found and avoided the result can be quite dramatic.

ADDITIVES AND DETERGENTS

In allergic reactions concerning food it is sometimes very difficult to know the part which may be played by additives and pesticides. It is a fact that literally thousands of chemical agents are employed in the preparation of various foods, especially where they have to be kept on shelves for varying periods of time, and there can be no doubt that people react to them in different ways so that we may be blaming a particular food when the additive may be the factor responsible. The same difficulty applies even to the natural foods, the fruits and vegetables which may have been treated with pesticides and other chemicals during their cultivation. The use of D.D.T. was an example of the danger of the use of some chemicals before their nature and effects were fully understood. Here, again, people may react quite differently since individuality is a very real thing with each person reacting in his own particular manner.

We can, of course, carry the allergy possibility still further and realize that the use of detergents may cause adverse reactions with some people. It is well known that detergents will sometimes cause intensive irritation on the hands and arms; how likely is it then that it may cause irritation in colitis with its hypersensitivity of the mucous membranes of the bowel. Milk may also be contaminated with penicillin so that in the experiments to determine its effects in colitis the drug might have also been at fault. Other animal products, meat and chicken, and so on, may not be free of hormones

WHAT CAUSES COLITIS? 33

that are used in their management by farmers and others. In short, food pollution is a fact of life, and sufferers from colitis will have to exercise a great deal of thought and discretion about their food and eating habits.

The question of infection as a cause of colitis, especially of the ulcerative kind, have been in the minds of medical researchers over the years, and from time to time affirmative reports have been made about the discovery of specific agents, so much so that at one time claims were made that preventive vaccine might be a possibility. Further experiments, however, have disproved this contention which is no longer regarded as valid. On the other hand, the general view seems to be that neither bacteria nor parasites are the primary cause of ulcerative colitis, and this view is further substantiated on the grounds that no form of drug treatment is effective as a cure.

If we accept this view of the complaint it gives validity to the notion that there may be such a possibility as prevention. Obviously, if we think that it arises purely through the activity of bacteria the chances of avoiding it are minimal and we should feel almost fatalistic about it; but, on the other hand, if the bacteria become active in a secondary way and only when the body defences have become weakened, then this puts a very different complexion on the whole subject. In short, the best prevention of illness and the activity of bacteria lies in sound nutrition and good health which, in the nature of things, must reside in adequate and wholesome food combined with other environmental needs and mental and emotional stability. In other words, in every form of illness, including colitis, the idea that it can be entirely caused by bacteria, or that it is purely a local affair is a misunderstanding of its real nature.

DIET REFORM

We have dealt at some length with the various ideas about the possible causative factors of colitis and it must now be evident that no one has been able to come up with a specific causative agent which might lead to a specific cure. This has not been due to a lack of time since, the complaint has been with us for a very long time and a good many medical researchers have paid a great deal of attention to it; but seeing that it is a complaint affecting so many people the need to have a better understanding of its cause or causes is a matter of real concern. If, however, the Nature Cure interpretation of its causes are along the right lines then we are entitled to take a more optimistic view of it. For if it is, as claimed, a complaint that owes its origin largely to the use of the foods which have become an integral part of industrial societies, then the fact must be faced that radical diet reform must take place if the illness is to be prevented. From that point of view its causes are closely associated with those which cause constipation so that to a great extent we must see that colitis is the result of the mismanagement of constipation.

The proper management of constipation means the adoption of food used as nearly as possible in its natural state of which, of course, fresh fruits, salads and vegetables are the main items. By so doing the body is supplied with all the essential elements necessary for its nutrition, including the vitamins, mineral salts, and — so far as constipation is concerned — the vitally important fibre without which the bodily system cannot function properly.

5.
Understanding the Symptoms

It is very important to try to understand the symptoms of any particular form of illness. Symptoms are regarded as the characteristic sign of disease, and by recognizing them in this way it becomes possible to make a diagnosis. There are many different kinds of symptoms, of course, and the most common ones are headache, fever, pain, nausea, vomiting, constipation, diarrhoea and so on. The symptoms are not, of course, the disease, and although this may seem an elementary thing to say, it is very important to keep the point in mind when planning treatment, since by confining treatment to symptoms it may be that important underlying causative factors may be missed. As a matter of fact a great deal of treatment by medicine is directed against symptoms. For example, there are those that are used for headaches, there are those that are employed to reduce fever, to counteract nausea, to treat constipation by laxatives, to stop diarrhoea and so on. In fact by far the greater number of medicines used today, and especially those used in self-medication, are used to suppress symptoms in one way or another, but do little or nothing in getting to the root of the matter or to have any real beneficial effect on the basic cause of the illness.

UNDERSTANDING SYMPTOMS
It has already been pointed out that constipation is one of the main symptoms of colitis in its early stages, and precious time is often lost

by the treatment of it by the use of laxative remedies instead of regarding it as a symptom of the disturbed function of the bowel caused by the use of food that has been too refined and deprived of the elements necessary for the natural elimination of the waste products from the body. This is a good example of where the treatment of a symptom, while overlooking a basic cause of illness may allow it to progress from one stage to another until the chronic condition has been established. The lesson here is clear that we should always try to understand each symptom as it arises in illness and not merely try to suppress it by the use of some remedy as is so often done at the present time.

HAEMORRHOIDS

No one can be really healthy so long as this important function of the body is in a disordered state, and what is worse, of course, is that further disorders will follow in its wake. But not the least important will be the difficulty in the evacuation of the waste products and the straining at stool. The most likely result of this will be the formation of haemorrhoids or piles, which will also set in motion more symptoms. Straining in this way will cause dilation of the terminal veins in the rectum which will possibly result in bleeding piles which may expose the tissues to the first stages of infection, possibly ending up with ulceration. Piles in themselves may be very painful, but they may also affect nearby nerves and thus gives rise to pain in the back and in other parts of the pelvic region of the body. Other symptoms may appear with the constipation, including headaches, and if these are treated with the usual remedies they may adversely affect the stomach and interfere with digestion. Aspirin is a good example of a remedy that in some susceptible people may cause congestion of the mucous membranes of the alimentary canal with the possibility of haemorrhage among other difficulties. Those who are susceptible to catarrh will know that it becomes more troublesome when the bowel is not functioning properly with colds and other such ailments suffered with much more frequency.

Occasionally bouts of diarrhoea, which usually attends chronic constipation, will indicate that the first step has been taken in the development of colitis in its simplest form.

All these changes may take place because there has not been a proper understanding of the symptom which is the manifestation of the underlying factor, in this case the use of unsuitable food. To attribute so much importance to constipation is not by any means a new suggestion: about a hundred years ago Dr Robert Bell, towards the end of a long active life in the practice of medicine and surgery wrote: '... the longer I have lived I have become more and more convinced that there exists no more potent factor in the production of disease than neglecting the daily evacuation ... there is no doubt whatever that chronic constipation, not only exercises a baneful effect upon one's general health, but, moreover, is responsible to a supreme extent for the development of gout, rheumatism, anaemia, and, to a marked degree, cancer; besides other blood affections of various types.' He went on to say that 'we should confine our diet to those articles which Nature has provided so amply for our use, which clearly indicates that they should consist of the fruits and vegetables of the earth. Then we should find that there would be no more constipation to give us trouble.'

ROUGHAGE

This is of some historical as well as medical interest, seeing that now, a century later, medical men who have spent some time in Africa studying the bowel habits of the inhabitants have come to the conclusion that many of the diseases from which many people living in industrial societies may suffer are largely due to a lack of 'roughage' or fibre in the refined, over-concentrated and convenience foods which form the main portion of their diet. They have linked to this fact conditions like constipation, diverticulitis, and even colon cancer, a similar conclusion reached by Dr Bell, who, after years of operating on this dread disease maintained that the natural foods that would make constipation a complaint of the past and also provide people with the best hope of preventing cancer and in some cases helping to overcome it. At least the one part of Dr Bell's thesis has been acknowledged; will the second one on cancer be one day fulfilled? Apart from any such speculation the evidence of Dr Bell and the other doctors mentioned above shows how important it is that constipation, caused by dietetic errors, should be recognized for what it is: a positive danger to health and a possible causative factor in many forms of ill health, including colitis.

If no radical change has been made after the simpler form of colitis has developed, and if the causative factors still remain, with perhaps only palliative treatment to keep the patient relatively comfortable, the illness will most likely progress to further changes and symptoms. With the continuing irritation of the bowel it will mean that the looseness of it will entail several or more evacuations during the day and night, and with this development will come the passing of varying quantities of mucus with the stools. The stage will then have been reached when the term mucous colitis will be used to describe it. Not surprisingly the sufferer will be psychologically upset, self-centred and depressed about his condition; so much so that some authorities have suggested that the illness is more of a psychosomatic nature than anything else, although one would have thought that so self-absorbing and distressing a condition could account for any mental upset that might accompany the illness.

By this time it will be evident that the complaint is by no means only a local one. With the digestive and bowel functions so disturbed the deterioration of the patient's general health will show in sallowness of the complexion, anaemia and a generally depressed physical state. Like other chronic conditions the complaint may have quiescent periods when the trouble appears to have abated for awhile. Relief from tension, worry and strain may help to bring a quiet period just as a very peaceful and pleasant holiday may have the same effect. It is often, in these periods, that an incident like an emotional upset or some unexpected bad news will almost immediately set the complaint going again, showing that it has only been a temporary cessation: the quick response to a psychological crisis shows how tense and 'on edge' the patient is and the close relationship between the psyche and the physical.

ULCERATIVE COLITIS

Ulcerative colitis is, of course, the complaint in its most serious form. The simplest analogy that can be given of it is to liken it to eczema on the skin. The list of symptoms accompanying the illness is quite formidable, and vividly illustrates the reason for the anxiety of the sufferer: diarrhoea, constipation, passing of mucus and blood, possibly elevation of temperature, stomach upsets, loss of weight, pains in the abdomen and in the rectum and anus. The symptoms may vary, of course, with each individual and in some cases there may be periods when the complaint goes through a stage that gives less trouble only to flare up again, apparently for no particular reason, adding again to the patient's dismay and despair. The most depressing symptom is naturally the frequency of the bowel movement which may be a dozen times or more during the day and night, thus adding to the trouble by interfering with the sleep and rest and making deeper inroads into the patient's stock of nervous energy.

The infection may vary in each case. In some very severe ones it may involve the whole of the colon, while there are some cases in which the lower bowel is mainly affected: this is sometimes spoken of as proctitis. Although the large bowel is chiefly involved in the illness, and its function so drastically disturbed, it is a mistake to think that the rest of the body is not involved in one way or another. It is usual to find that a person suffering from ulcerative colitis suffers also from what is known as systemic disorders in which other parts and organs are affected. The blood may certainly be affected and consequently the nutrition of the whole system will be below par. The drain on the resources of the body is fairly certain to cause anaemia, a cause of which might also be a loss of blood in the stools. Ulcers in the mouth is a commonly related symptom, and the eyes may also be affected; iritis is a troublesome complication. Rashes may appear on the skin and, in some cases, the joints may become almost arthritic. These facts make it clear that ulcerative colitis is by no means just a local disorder of the bowel; it is, in fact, more of the nature of a generalized disease. It is probably much wiser to take this view of the illness since it will help the patient to understand that in treatment much more must be involved than the mere palliation of the bowel disorder: the whole person is ill and nothing less than the restoration of full general health must be the aim. The picture of the ulcerative colitic patient is that of a very debilitated person whose digestion, nutrition and energy has been thoroughly depleted — a picture that one might justly deplore since if the complaint had been caught in the early stages and a radical change made in the diet so much illness might have been prevented. This view was amply confirmed by a Harvard professor, who, writing in *A Layman's Handbook of Medicine*, said that in his experience of early types of colitis 'the important remedies were rest, warmth and starvation'. By starvation he meant fasting, that is, the withholding of food for therapeutic purposes.

SEVERE ULCERATION

There is no gainsaying the fact that a severe case of ulcerative colitis is a very serious illness. One has only to think of the damage to the walls and mucous membranes of the bowel to realize how much it must interfere with normal function and how it must spread its dire effects right throughout the system. Generally speaking, the infection and other changes in the mucous mebranes start in the lower end of the bowel and move upward. The infection is preceded by congestion and inflammation of the mucous membranes — the time when early treatment would have been effective — and this is followed by the irritation of the passage of the waste products. No doubt the constipation, with its dry and hardened faeces, has helped to cause the congestion and inflammation in the first place, and from then onward it must keep up a constant irritation and it is

UNDERSTANDING THE SYMPTOMS

this irritation that promotes the excessive secretion of the mucus which is usually so alarming to the patient. The mucous membranes naturally become more sensitive, and if there is no change in the condition, or if no effective treatment is commenced, the formation of the ulcers may begin. A medical writer in describing the condition offers the following analogy: 'The situation may be compared to a first degree burn of the skin upon which a poultice of faeces has been placed. Inevitably infection and ulceration will follow.' The situation is also fraught with great difficulties and problems. The patient must eat and the end products of digestion will have to pass along the damaged and ulcerated mucous membranes constantly making matters much worse.

Once the complaint has reached the ulcerative stage it naturally becomes self-perpetuating. At first small ulcers will form; these develop into larger ones that will coalesce with each other. There may, in some cases, be the formation of small polyps (small tumour-like bodies). At first, the ulcers are limited to the mucous membranes but with further development the walls of the bowel may be affected and there is then the danger of perforation. The condition is further complicated by infection and the activity of bacteria and possibly some parasites – complications one might expect when the tissues and the blood have lost their protective qualities. When the complaint has reached this stage we may be sure that much medical treatment has been tried in an effort to contain the illness. In medical terms, to control rather than to 'cure' is the main idea. For this purpose various drugs will have been used, with bedrest in the early days of the trouble, and, so far as diet is concerned, the use of milk will have been forbidden and psychotherapy will have been used in some cases. If these measures fail to control the complaint it may go on to surgery. In this case the surgeon may be called upon to remove the whole or part of the colon; if this is done an artificial opening has to be made in the abdominal wall for the removal of the faeces. It is clear, then, that the individual should try to do all in his power to overcome his complaint and thus save himself from the discomforts which surgery may bring.

6.
Self-Help Treatment for Colitis

The reader having followed the discussion as far as this will understand some of the essential facts about the nature of the complaint and realize why so much emphasis has been placed on constipation, and its treatment by laxative medicines, as the important factor both as the cause of the illness and as a constant irritating danger in the later stages when serious ulcerative developments may have taken place. This knowledge will, of course, clearly indicate to the reader that the condition, out of which constipation arises, is the use of food which has not provided the body with the necessary elements for the carrying out of its normal functions. And the failure of a function so important as the elmination of waste products would inevitably have disastrous consequences, and clearly no medicine can possibly be a substitute for proper food. It follows, that, unless proper food is chosen, the general health will be at risk and a breakdown almost inevitable. The danger at the present time, and this is true of all industrial societies, is that the food which is now so readily available has been so refined and denatured that it is deficient in quality, though quite adequate in quantity. A person may satisfy his appetite and hunger while living on these highly processed and convenience foods and yet find himself ill-fed and liable to suffer from illnesses like colitis. If we are to find ways in which these troubles may be prevented, or overcome, we must find better ways of nourishing the body, which will mean returning to the more natural foods, the fruits and vegetables, and to make use of them, as far as possible in their natural state.

SIMPLE COLITIS

Simple colitis is not a very clearly defined illness but it is a condition that is often neglected and likely to develop into more serious trouble if it is. As a rule it affects those who have suffered, on and off, from constipation for some time and treated it rather casually with the usual household remedies under the impression that it was of no particular importance. Having obtained relief from laxatives, no attention has been paid to the diet which consisted of food mainly in tins and packages. It is only when pain and discomfort make themselves felt that the individual becomes aware that all is not well and an attack of diarrhoea will make him more anxious about it. What has happened, of course, is that the bowel, from the use of the laxatives and the lack of 'roughage' in the diet has become irritated and possibly slightly inflamed which results in the periodic attacks of the diarrhoea. The sufferer, probably of a nervous temperament, starts to worry about the condition and this makes matters worse. An attack of haemorrhoids, which may accompany this, will add to the problem and the anxiety.

In such cases one may be quite sure that the individual will begin to look around for some kind of medicine that helps him to overcome his trouble, and if he is unfortunate enough to find a powerful one that will suppress the symptoms of the complaint he will be in a much more perilous position. For if the cause of the trouble has not been removed the adverse effects on the body will continue, and, in addition drugs may produce side-effects to complicate the issue. The trouble will not be confined to the bowel by this time since the disturbed function of it will set up reactions in other parts of the digestive tract making itself felt in indigestion, catarrhal conditions and so on.

People who may suffer in this way are very often those who are in sedentary occupations, or who sit in cars for long periods and who tend to be physically inactive. Consequently, they usually have slack and flabby abdominal muscles, and the possibility of congestion in the lower parts of the body is very great, and a not unusual accompaniment of constipation is varicose veins. The lack of exercise may cause trouble, not only in the superficial muscles of the body, arms and the limbs, and so on, but also in the structures of the internal organs, and we should remember that all movements in the body, as well as the movement of the body involves the use of muscular tissues. The slackness of the abdominal muscles may be reflected in the movement of the bowel and may be an important factor in the causation of colitis.

TREATMENT OF SIMPLE COLITIS

The proper and effective treatment in cases of this kind does not lie in the further use of medicine but a radical overhauling of the dietetic habits, and the adoption of more and suitable exercise. This will naturally call for will-power and self-discipline. If the diarrhoea attacks have been fairly persistent a start should be made by resting the digestive organs. A twenty-four to thirty-six hour period on unsweetened fruit juice, if possible at a weekend when it will not interfere with the ordinary occupation, will be very helpful and will have a beneficial effect on the diarrhoea. This should be followed by a fruit diet consisting of fresh ripe fruit, apples and grapes being especially useful. The use of fruit at such a time may be contrary to some people's ideas about the value of such an article of diet when the bowel action is upset, but the experiment — by no means an experiment in nature cure practice — will soon convince the sufferer of the soothing and cleansing value of it at such a time.

The fruit diet should be continued for a further day or two for its beneficial effect on the whole of the digestive system, since it is the best way of correcting acidity of the stomach, overcoming nausea and catarrh, conditions which are usually associated with constipation. The fruit diet should be followed by a diet in which natural foods will play a dominant part. The fruits, salads and vegetables should be included in the daily meals, and a plan, which seems to suit most people, is to use fresh and dried fruit, together with a wholegrain product such as wholewheat bread for breakfast, and at midday a salad made with all kinds of raw, edible vegetables, with two or three nicely cooked vegetables for the evening meal. If more convenient the midday and evening meal foods may be reversed. Other foods, meat, fish, cheese, eggs, and so on may be added in moderate quantities, but the main point to bear in mind is that the natural foods carry with them the fibre and other elements which will assist elimination and must on no account be omitted from the diet. In addition to the use of natural foods, it is essential that during the day two or three glasses of water must be taken which will help to limit the too free use that is generally made of tea and coffee and other beverages. It may take a little time for the body to adjust to this plan; in some cases there may be a little flatulence but this will soon right itself. If bowel movement seems to be delayed no laxative must be taken and the bowel must be allowed to adjust itself. The important thing is to allow the new diet to have its good effect which it will definitely do if the patient is willing to leave the regulation to the body itself.

EXERCISE

A great help will be the adoption of more exercise that will activate the whole system, including, of course, the circulation which is so important in keeping all parts supplied with nutriment and in removing the waste products of cell life. At least there should be a daily brisk walk and if one is on the young side a little jogging shakes up the abdominal organs to good effect. A good corrective exercise that will directly stimulate bowel activity is done as follows: get down on the floor on the knees and the elbows and then move the body backward and forward from ten to twenty times. A good time to do the exercise is just before retiring so as to counteract the effects of the sitting position which may have been prolonged during the day.

Overcoming constipation and colitis before they develop into the chronic stage is a safeguard for the future and the best health investment that anyone can make.

TREATMENT OF MUCOUS COLITIS

This form of colitis is characterized by the passing of the stools of large or lesser amounts of mucus. There may be other symptoms such as stabbing pains in the abdominal region together with attacks of constipation and diarrhoea and continuously loose bowel motions. It is sometimes spoken of as an irritable colon, since there are remissions occasionally when the complaint seems quiet and the bowel function is relatively normal. It is a very trying illness so far as the patient is concerned and also sometimes very trying for the person who is treating it. The patient is generally very upset, which some authorities maintain is the cause of the complaint. In a medical text it says that 'there is fairly general agreement that the complaint is largely, if not entirely, psychosomatic in nature'. It is sometimes said to be associated with a spastic colon and in such a case there is more likely to be more pain and discomfort whereas in other cases there may be very little pain. The effect of the complaint on the general health is very marked; it may be very poor indeed, with sallow skin, listless manner and general malaise. It is generally assumed that women, particularly middle aged ones, are the most liable to suffer from this distressing complaint and patients may become almost obsessional about the bowel function.

RESTING THE SYSTEM

The patient should be persuaded to try to ignore, as far as possible, the activity of the bowel and endeavour to concentrate on the idea of improving the health of the whole body — foregoing any previously held notion that all attention should be centred on the colon and the mucus. A definite period of rest, for both mind and body, is called for in such cases and it should be made as thorough as

SELF-HELP TREATMENT FOR COLITIS 47

possible. A few days in bed when starting the treatment will be very helpful and at such a time the digestive organs should be rested as well. No solid food should be taken; limit yourself to hot lemon drinks, sweetened with a little honey (but no sugar) together with other fruit juices which may be freely taken. Resting the functions of the body in this way will ease the mind also, and every effort should be made to induce both mental and physical relaxation. Sufferers from this complaint are invariably tense and anxious and they need, above all things, to learn to 'let go'. They should try to relax all their muscles as much as possible by conscious effort.

During the resting period, a comfortably hot bath should be taken each day and it should be done to assist in the relieving of the tense muscles. Some people find it easier to relax in water than otherwise, and, if this is so, in any particular case, the bath may be used both in the morning and in the evening. The patient may be sure that the illness will benefit almost in ratio to the amount of relaxation that has been achieved. The benefit of the relaxation will be shown also in the more refreshing sleep that the patient will enjoy. Colitic sufferers are prone to feelings of anxiety, worry and fears and relaxation is the best antidote to them. If the resting period and the relaxation procedures have been successful in easing the situation, the patient may feel it worthwhile to carry on for a day or two longer, and that would be a very good thing to do, especially if there are sympathetic friends who would give encouragement.

Having thoroughly rested and relaxed the mind and body in this way, thought must now be given to the diet to follow the resting period. The orthodox treatment is based on the idea of a diet that is lacking in residue, and the avoidance of any food that might irritate the colon. Here is just such a prescription as taken from a medical text: 'The diet must not be irritating; no foods leaving residue should be eaten; no salads, skins of fruit or fish or pips must be taken.' A person who may have been following such a diet will have to make a considerable mental adjustment to accept the idea that a change to more natural food is required if the trouble is to be overcome and the normal function restored to the colon. However, one good thing has happened recently and that is the publicity that has been given by some doctors to the idea that fibre (residue) is essential for the normal function of the bowel, which has led to the popular use of bran.

DIET

The diet to follow the resting period should be carefully graduated. As the condition is basically catarrhal it will be advisable to avoid, in the early stages of the dieting, the dairy products, and to rely more on the fruit and vegetables. The first meal of the day should consist of fruit: apples are especially useful in all disorders of the colon. If the patient has good teeth and is able to masticate the fruit may be eaten normally; otherwise it should be grated and eaten with a spoon. The midday meal should be baked potatoes with an evening meal of ripe bananas. These meals should be taken for a couple of days and then enlarged by adding fruits at breakfast, a little tender salad, such as the heart of lettuce, to the midday meal: the evening meal should consist of potatoes and other cooked vegetables.

By this time the easing of the bowel motions and the lessening of the catarrh will have made the patient less fearful of using the natural foods; the selection of foods may then be on a wider scale. Breakfast should consist of at least one kind of fruit, together with, perhaps, one or two slices of wholewheat bread and a little butter, which must be very well chewed. Lunch should consist of some tender salad with a potato dish, the potato being one of the most valuable of the carbohydrate foods; it increases the alkalinity of the blood and tissues and has greater food value than many people are aware of. It has special value in the present case. The evening meal should be of cooked vegetables, to which an egg dish, lean meat or white fish may be added. The vegetarian will substitute a suitable protein food. As a rule, it is wise to keep to a one-course meal in the early stages of the treament; later on fruit of various kinds may be used as dessert.

In addition to the careful selection and use of suitable foods it is very important to keep up the resting periods and the practice of conscious relaxation until the general health has been improved. One must remember that colitis affects the whole system much more than many people think and conversely, poor health will impoverish blood and the tissues which will impede the healing processes. These processes depend on good food and good nutrition which it promotes, but other factors are also important. Adequate rest and sleep are vital to the well-being of the mind and body.

FRESH AIR

When people are ill they are inclined to forget the importance of fresh air and exercise; remaining indoors and riding in cars may make this very difficult to obtain. Yet both are necessary to good health: the lungs need the air to oxygenate the blood and the muscles need the exercise to maintain their tone. There are no real substitutes for good food, fresh air and exercise, all of which are essential to keep the mind and body in health, and especially so in illness and its management. A complaint like colitis may seem to be concentrated in the colon, but in fact the whole person and personality is involved and must be fully considered in the 'getting well' process.

It is important to stress the point that no medicine of any kind should be used when semi-fasting or following a fairly strict diet. No medicine is safe and will produce side-effects in some measure; when the body is treated along natural lines it may be intensified and it is unwise therefore to take the risk. Nature Cure treatment is based on the Hippocratic idea that all healing comes from within the body and efforts are made through rest, fasting, and the regulation of the digestive process to improve nutrition and thus conserve the vital energy for the purpose of healing and the regaining of health. Medicine cannot be a substitute for natural healing; it may relieve pain, suppress symptoms and possibly change the pattern of disease, but it cannot heal in the true sense of the word. Only nature cures.

A CASE HISTORY

Miss S, 53, had suffered for many years from mucous colitis. She was a tall, very slender type of person, drawn and rather haggard in appearance, with, it seemed, very little mental or physical energy. She was almost completely self-centered with very little interest outside her own restricted life. She was very nervous, which plainly showed in her general attitude and the twitching movements of her hands and eyes. She appeared to be full of fears, above all, the fear of taking any kind of food that might be irritating to the bowel. She had in the past been under medical care and it seemed that she was advised to follow a bland diet as the best way of coping with her complaint, and, in fact, she had been given very little medicine. She had taken the advice quite literally, arranging her diet so that there was practically no residue. It consisted largely of milk and eggs and dishes made from them. Rice pudding made with white rice, of course, and white bread, since she was afraid that brown bread would be irritating. She was quite fearful of the idea that she might swallow pips or seeds, so that ruled out strawberries and raspberries and so on. When she did go out for tea or for any kind of meal she would try to make sure that the cake did not contain caraway seeds, and tomatoes were out of the question. In short, it had become not merely a whim but almost her whole purpose in life.

She had come to Nature Cure, rather unwillingly, through the advice of a friend who was very anxious to help her. It was almost impossible to persuade the patient that her diet was a mistaken one, and that it was necessary to include fruit, salads and vegetables in it if she was ever to regain normal bowel motion and improve her general health. It become only possible to get her to try the treatment by virtue of the fact that her friend volunteered to stay with her and help her to do so. Fortunately, her friend was a very practical person, who seemed to have a natural aptitude for caring for sick people, and also one able to instil confidence. She superintended the resting period and was most helpful in the carrying out of the relaxing measures which in this case were so important. She also had experience with the use of enema, which she was able to employ to clear and activate the lower bowel; in addition she knew how to make effective use of hot fomentations which she used to good effect to relieve the painful cramps from which the patients suffered from time to time. All these things helped her to gain the confidence of her friend, and thus to persuade her to gain control over her fears and tensions and to rest and relax more fully. In the same way she was able to get the dietetic instructions properly carried out.

Progress was made step by step, with the patient taking much more interest in herself and in the treatment, and after some weeks of treatment, it was clear that with patience and persistence it would end in real success. With the improvement the patient's personality seemed to take on a new image; with the increase in energy she began to take more interest in things outside her own home, with trips to the theatre and short walks in the country. And best of all, she was much less fearful and anxious about things which in the past had been so large a part of her life. What it demonstrated, perhaps more than anything else, was the effectiveness of good nursing and the sympathetic interest taken in her case by her friend. Of course the diet and the other forms of treatment were essential for success, but the determining factor was the friend's insistence and help.

TREATMENT OF ULCERATIVE COLITIS

Ulcerative colitis is, of course, the most serious form of colitis. It is a chronic condition, with the formation of ulcers affecting the mucous membranes of the colon. There is no known specific cause of it but many factors have come under suspicion. It is considered by some authorities to be caused by food allergies; milk, wheat and other foods have been tested with that idea in view, but so far milk seems to be the most likely culprit. As with other forms of colitis the psychological factor is an important aspect to be dealt with, both when considering causes and when planning treatment. While it is generally regarded as a disease which affects adults, it may sometimes be seen in quite young people. It starts with attacks of diarrhoea, and abdominal pains which may be severe enough to resemble appendicitis. The diarrhoea will continue and there will be mucus and blood in the stools. Its continuation will, of course, interfere with nutrition so that the patient will become anaemic, lose weight and energy. There may be slight fever in some cases, and, as the illness develops, other parts of the body will suffer, including the joints and the mucous membranes in the mouth. If nothing is done to arrest the complaint it will run on to the chronic form assuming the condition of a generalized disease, the serious and intractable nature of which no one will doubt. That it is a very difficult illness to deal with is plainly admitted by medical authorities who declare that it may need prolonged treatment, and even then with liability to relapse. Medical treatment involves the use of powerful drugs, the serious side effects of which are plainly recognized; the diet generally prescribed stresses the need for a low residue, which excludes the natural foods. Milk is generally proscribed, together with the exclusion of fruit and salads.

From the view of Nature Cure the treatment must involve a most radical change, not only of food, but also of almost every aspect of the daily life of the sufferer. Nothing less than a total health-building programme must be instituted that will take into consideration everything that can be done to build up the resistance of the body so as to effectively combat the infectious process. Every effort must be made to afford the patient relief as early as possible, and this may be done by a thorough rest of mind and body to compensate for the drainage of nervous energy that has been undergone. The next important thing is to rest the digestive organs and this may be done by semi-fasting measures. Such patients are usually weakened and debilitated by the illness, so that a complete fast, that is, on water only, would not be advisable. The next best thing is a fruit fast and experience has shown that the apple is the best fruit to use. It is not as acid as the citrus fruits which might not be tolerated quite so well in the early stages of the treatment. The apples should be ripe and of the sweeter kind, and they should be rubbed through the grater to remove most of the skin. The pulp and the juice should then be eaten with a spoon. It should be taken three or four times during the day and during the resting period which may be carried on for three or four days, depending on the patient's strength and willingness to do so. In most cases the relief given by this simple diet will give the sufferer so much relief that it is usually not very difficult to get the cooperation that is necessary.

The use of the enema to clear the lower bowel may be very helpful at this time, but in some cases it is not easy to arrange for its use. Some years ago this appliance could be bought at almost any chemist shop and the use of it is so simple that it could be used by the individual himself. But for some reason or other it now seems difficult to obtain – possibly due to the present idea that there is a pill for everything. In the circumstances, it might be possible to get it done locally, and if so, about a pint of warm water should be injected into the lower bowel for cleansing purposes. This should be done each day in the early stages of the treatment for two or three days. It should be remembered that the illness greatly depletes the energy of the sufferer and a loss of energy means that there is difficulty in keeping warm, and warmth is essential during the treatment. The feet may be cold when in bed, and this must be remedied by the use of the hot water bottle or the electric pad. The daily comfortably hot bath is a great help in this respect, and should be indulged in at least once a day, since this is also a valuable asset in helping to relax the tensions from which patients are liable to suffer. Relaxation is, of course, just as important as rest and sleep and the more that it can be induced the better the results will be. The psychological aspect of the illness should always be kept in mind, especially in the early stages, and often the individual may help himself by going over the anxieties and worries that he may have and endeavouring to get them into proper perspective.

If there are painful and possibly cramping spasms in the abdomen use should be made of hot fomentations. They are very effective in giving relief and are simple to use, and as no pain-killing drugs should be used at this time, they are a good and reliable substitute. A piece of material is wrung out in hot water and applied to the lower abdomen and well covered with dry material to retain the heat. This may be repeated several times a day, and it will be found that even if there are no pains the use of the hot fomentations will have a very beneficial effect on the colon and the other internal organs. In some cases a cold compress may be used after the hot fomentations to stimulate the circulation, but this must only be done if the patient is strong enough to get a proper reaction to it. Some patients find it very refreshing and it is worth a trial if there is no objection to it.

GRADUATION TO SOLID FOODS

When the early stage of the treatment has been gone through careful thought must be given to the next stage, which will involve the use of more solid foods. Here, then, is an outline of the diet that should follow: *First Meal:* grated apple, as before, to which may be added a raw, ripe banana. If desired, a baked apple may be taken in place of the grated one. *Lunch:* the best carbohydrate food for this illness is the potato and baked ones should be used but without the skin in the early days. However, it should be noted that no salt, butter or gravy should be used. And here, it might be remarked, that a baked potato, retaining as it does its full food value, as distinct from those that have been peeled and boiled in possibly salt water, is a much more complete food than many people imagine. Although essentially a carbohydrate food, it does supply the body with a certain amount of protein. *Evening Meal:* two cooked vegetables, potatoes, carrots or other suitable ones; baked apples. Unsweetened apple juice may be taken as a beverage, and occasionally a cup of weak tea, with a slice of lemon but no milk or sugar.

This very austere diet should be followed for two days before the diet is gradually enlarged, and it should be pointed out that in keeping to a strictly limited diet the idea is to be sure that the residue of it will not cause any irritation to the already irritated and ulcerated bowel. In so doing, it is giving the infected parts a chance to heal, whereas, of course, if the residue contained toxic substances from a more mixed diet, containing perhaps animal products, it would most likely have the reverse effect.

By this time relief and improvement will be evident: the pains and discomfort will have diminished and the stools will be fewer and more formed. The next step will be to further enlarge the diet but one must proceed very slowly, and at this time the different foods that may be added should be watched for any signs of allergic reactions. If any kind of food appears to adversely affect the colon it should, of course, be omitted, at least for the time being.

Breakfast: This should be of fruit and still include apples which are particularly valuable in all bowel complaints; other fruits bananas, grapes (omitting pips), peaches, oranges and other fruits that may be available.

Lunch: Two cooked vegetables. Baked potatoes, baked apples.

Evening: Very much the same as lunch with cooked brown rice or oats.

After this diet has been carried out for a few days the patient should be feeling much more confident about himself so that a start may be made on more of the natural foods, keeping in mind, as mentioned before, the question of allergy, noting after the inclusion of any different food whether any particular reaction has occurred. The following basic menus will give an idea of the normal diet to adopt:

Breakfast: Various fruits including apples and bananas. Muesli or wholewheat bread with a little honey, both to be well masticated.

Lunch: Baked potatoes. Salad of lettuce, avocado, grated carrots, dressed with vegetable oil and lemon. Minimum of sea salt. Baked apple to follow.

Evening meal: Two cooked vegetables. An egg dish. Apple baked or raw and other fruit if desired.

After a week or so of this diet the addition of other foods may be considered. It will have been noticed that milk and other dairy products have been omitted, and, generally speaking, milk, is to be avoided. On the other hand it may be worthwhile giving yogurt a trial since, if it is tolerated, it could be a very useful addition to either of the meals. If it is found that yogurt can be tolerated then the next food to try would be cottage cheese and, again, if it brings no adverse reactions, add it to your diet with eggs and yogurt.

It will be seen that meat and fish have been excluded from the diet, and one's experience in these cases is that a non-flesh diet is the best plan — at least, for a considerable period after the bowel has regained its normal function. The reason for this is to make sure that the residue of food which has to pass through the colon is as non-toxic as possible. When a person is on a non-flesh diet the stools will differ in many ways from that of the meat eater. They will be paler in colour and less offensive, and, in passing over the infected part of the colon, will be less liable to irritate and add to the infection — a very important consideration.

ALLOW THE BODY TO CURE ITSELF

The reader may wonder, perhaps, why so much emphasis is placed on the importance of the dietary factor in the treatment of this illness, but it shows very clearly the essential difference between the Nature Cure method of treating this complaint and that of the medical profession. By semi-fasting, resting the digestive organs, improving nutrition and conserving the vital energy, the body is given the best possible chance to cure itself — which, is, of course, in accordance with the idea of natural healing. On the other hand, the orthodox treatment relies more on the use of drugs and does not insist on a rigid and limited plan of diet. To illustrate the point here is a lunch meal as set out in a medical text book in its advice about food in the treatment of ulcerative colitis: 'Lunch. A choice of: Cream of vegetable soup, lean tender meat, rabbit, chicken, sweetbreads, kidneys, white fish (grilled, baked or steamed) mashed or boiled potatoes, *purée* of vegetables, milk puddings, fruit *purée*, jelly, fruit juices, ripe bananas, mild cheese, toast, butter, cream.' It added 'that sugar may be taken as desired' and among the foods to be avoided were raw fruits and salads. In addition, the use of several drugs were advocated, and it was frank enough to say if these measures failed surgical ones would have to be considered.

While no one would argue that surgical measures were never necessary, there is no doubt that with all the inconvenience and discomfort which they entail in this complaint, the sufferer should be willing to make every effort and almost any sacrifice to avoid them, and certainly be willing to change the dietetic and other habits which may be essential for the restoration of his health and well-being. And, as we have already seen, this complaint does not affect only the bowel: the eyes, mouth and the joints, among other parts of the system, may be involved with dire consequences to them. So that in this illness, as with all other kinds, one should always take into consideration the assumption that the patient has the disease, and not, as is so often done, that the disease has the patient. From this standpoint, we see that man does not live by food alone: there are many other factors like the stresses and strains of daily habits, plus many other environmental factors which help to break down mental and physical resistance and lead to illnesses like colitis.

ASSOCIATED DISORDERS: THE JOINTS

We must, for instance, see the importance of daily exercise in maintaining the health and efficiency of the bodily system, which, in turn promotes the stability and integrity of mental well-being. The muscular system and the joints of the body play their part in general health and we see that in colitis the joints, in particular may be affected setting up a condition resembling arthritis. In cases where such a condition has developed direct help will have to be given for the restoration of the normal functioning of the joints and the muscles with which they are associated. The health of the joints and muscles depends upon movement to maintain the circulation which brings to them essential nutriments and remove from them the waste products of their activity. In colitis, the blood, being impoverished by the disease and possibly carrying toxic substances from the infected bowel, set up changes in the joint and muscular tissues just as they do in the eyes and in the formation of ulcers in the mouth. When the bowel function has again been restored and the residue of the digestion removed in the normal way, the joints and the other affected parts will return to normal, unless, of course, they have been structurally damaged. As far as the joint trouble is concerned, as soon as the colitis begins to improve efforts should be made to improve the joints as soon as possible. For this purpose an Epsom Salts bath, using about one pound to the bath, will be found to be very helpful. The bath should be reasonably hot and while in the bath the affected joints should be gently moved under the water. The bath should be taken two or three times a week. In some cases, where the hands and the fingers seem to be mainly affected, bathing them two or three times a day in hot water to which a handful of Epsom Salts has been added, will help to reduce the stiffness and mobilize the joints.

MUSCLES

Colitis, if it has been in existence over a prolonged period will weaken all the muscles in the body, especially those of the abdomen. Simple exercises like lying on the back on the floor and raising first the head and shoulders and then the legs just a few inches off the floor will contract and tighten these muscles and restore their tone. In addition, this exercise will directly affect the tissues and the circulation of the colon and help to restore them to a more normal condition. Equally important as exercise is relaxation, and the patients, even after the trouble has been overcome, must make a point of relaxing both mind and body so as to prevent further tensions building up.

INNER CALM

The psychological aspect of ulcerative colitis is regarded by all those who have had experience of it as a major factor to be kept in mind at all times, and if the patient should have to bear an extra burden involving emotional upsets, worry and anxiety of various kinds, apart from meeting these strains with understanding and fortitude, he should adjust his diet and relaxing exercises so as to preserve as much as possible his poise and nervous energy. At such times it is the building up of tensions that tend to sap the vitality and lead to a breakdown in health, and if the person is conscious of such a danger there is no doubt that much can be done to ameliorate the situation by adopting a more philosophic attitude towards life and its problems. It is important that those who have gone through an illness like ulcerative colitis should make themselves fully aware of the need to maintain an inner calm in the face of difficulties.

SELF-DISCIPLINE

In many ways this is a matter of self-discipline which is so necessary in all forms of self-help treatment. A person who may be willing to abstain from food and go on to a strict diet must involve himself in the proceedings. It is something calling for more responsibility than just getting a prescription or taking a drug. The individual must take an intelligent interest in himself and his complaint and be willing to exercise a good deal of self-control. On the other hand, in doing so, he builds up his own will-power and confidence which is an important asset in the management of any kind of illness. He realizes that he has to assume some responsibility for controlling factors which may be inimical to his health and well-being, and not just leave it for someone else to act for him. When Professor Ivan Illich declared that modern medicine had become a menace to health he was saying, in effect, that as individuals we have come to depend too much on medicine and in consequence, lost the ability to act for ourselves. This situation has been exploited more by the makers of medicines than by those who prescribe them and thus a great industry has grown up with large commercial interests and widespread advertising capacities so that few individuals have the will to resist the menace that Professor Illich talks about. The weakness in his argument is that he offers little in the way of a substitute which can only be met by Nature Cure and the self-help theory which it expounds. No other illness confirms the need for self-help treatment more than colitis; if a satisfactory solution is to be found for it, it will be in this way.

DISPOSITION TO INFECTION

All forms of illness tend to affect those who are predisposed to them, and, of course, ulcerative colitis is no exception. As we have seen it is an infection of the colon, and although many people may suffer from other forms of colitis they do not suffer from an infection. In any infection there is some form of bacterial or parasitical activity which the resistance and natural safeguards of the body have failed to prevent. The body is, of course, well supplied with the means of resisting such an invasion; for example, a really healthy stomach with its powerful acid is able to destroy bacteria and other harmful organisms when they are taken into it and thus prevent them from entering into the lower intestines and other parts of the system where their activity may do great harm. On the other hand, the reverse is true of the unhealthy stomach, especially one that is catarrhal and unable to perform its normal function. For this reason people who have stomach disorders and are deficient in the supply of acid are liable to suffer from bowel troubles like ulcerative colitis, and indeed other forms of infection that affect the colon like cholera and even typhoid. These diseases are not caught: they are swallowed; that is to say, they enter the system by way of the mouth and infect the colon because in some people the stomach was not able to destroy the offending germ. Thus we see how important it is that the stomach is kept healthy by virtue of using suitable food and observing other hygienic practices.

This is even more important for those who are prone to infections such as ulcerative colitis, and they should, even after they have recovered from the illness, take special care to see that they are not re-infected. The healthy body is well protected against such infection, as we have seen, and when we think of the dangers which it has to meet in this way we can only wonder at its efficiency. Take for example, the dangers of our streets, fouled with dog dejecta which may be carried on shoes in homes, on to carpets where children may play, and yet, in the main, its potential for infection is curbed by the body. On the other hand those who are more susceptible to such infection may not escape, and they may be left wondering why they have suffered in this way, without, perhaps suspecting the cause. There is no doubt that a thoroughly healthy person is immune to many dangers of this kind, that may affect those who are not so well endowed and who must be more careful of themselves until they, too, have achieved a better standard of health and raised their powers of immunity.

PREVENTION IN THE FUTURE

Even when a sufferer has made a good recovery from colitis he should exercise care in the future to prevent recurrence, and there are several important points that he should bear in mind. If he should return to his previous eating habits he should realize that the greatest danger lies in the use of animal foods which are more likely to cause putrefaction, and are of course, the offending foods in most cases of food poisoning. This should be borne in mind when eating out in restaurants where one cannot be quite as sure as one may be in one's own home. The safest foods are undoubtedly the fruits, salads, vegetables and the whole grain ones which can make up an adequate diet. As we have seen milk is under a good deal of mistrust in this respect, and it would be wise for the individual to use it in small quantities and certainly not to make it a major item in his diet. Eggs and cheese are good protein foods but they should be used in moderation, and of course, condiments, salt, pepper, vinegar and so on should be used very sparingly, if at all. It stands to reason that those are the things which really irritate the colon and not the fibre or roughage that is found in natural foods. In fact, of course, as soon as the colon has regained its function and the infection has diminished the inclusion of fibre in the diet is a necessary preventive measure.

It seems almost unnecessary to say that as far as prevention is concerned constipation must be avoided by past sufferers of colitis, but if by chance it should occur it should not be treated with laxatives. In emergency, an enema should be used to give relief and then the diet should be adjusted to take care of the situation. Those who have suffered from colitis are more susceptible to harm being done by constipation than other people, and those who have recovered from ulcerative colitis will know that it has been a very hard task that has demanded much patience and persistence and, perhaps, a certain amount of sacrifice of time and effort, and they should not allow themselves to fall back into bad habits of eating, lack of rest and relaxation and indifference to the care which the healthy body demands, for it is certain that if the causative factors are allowed to operate again no one should be surprised if the trouble returns.

Other recommended books . . .

THE BROWN RICE COOKBOOK
DELICIOUS, WHOLESOME MACROBIOTIC RECIPES
Craig and Ann Sams. Brown rice is a wholesome, unadulterated, natural food with a flavour that polished white rice can never match; and of course, it is full of vitamins and fibre which are both essential for a healthy diet. This very useful addition to the kitchen bookshelf gives some 100 clearly presented, tasty and ingenious recipes that demonstrate the many ways in which this versatile food can be used.

HANSSEN'S COMPLETE CIDER VINEGAR
Maurice Hanssen. Describes how this unique folk medicine reduces over-weight by helping the body burn unwanted fat instead of storing it. The book also reveals its healing value for arthritis and rheumatism, nose and throat disorders, insomnia and asthma, shingles, high blood-pressure, varicose veins, hay fever, constipation, etc. *Other contents include:* How cider vinegar is made; Choosing the right cider vinegar; The composition of cider vinegar; How to employ cider vinegar in cooking — with a selection of tasty recipes; Cider vinegar for slimming; Cider vinegar in the treatment of sick animals.

HERBAL TEAS FOR HEALTH AND HEALING
Ceres. *Illustrated.* Over a hundred tea-making herbs are described in this delightful book. Some are slightly stimulating, others are tonics for restoring the system to complete health. Many can 'lift' melancholy and depression; others are nocturnal and daytime tranquillizers, and there are teas to alleviate pain and clear the skin, also herbal infusions for external uses as poultices and skin-tonics. *Includes:* Carminative teas 'for comforting the stomacke'; Cosmetic teas 'for helping to beautify the skin'; Pain-killing teas 'for allaying the agony'; Febrifuge teas 'to allay the fever'; Teas to induce sleep 'and to help settle obstreporous spirits'.

HOW TO EAT FOR HEALTH
DIET REFORM SIMPLIFIED
Stanley Lief N.D. An authority on the question of dietetics, Stanley Lief maintained that the fundamental truths of scientific diet are unchangeable. In this book he has embodied the most important information necessary for those who wish to eat wisely, know when to eat, how much to eat, what to eat, and the most healthful method of preparing their food. All these vital facts are presented by the author in simple, succinct language. Over seventy mouth-watering recipes are included. *Other contents:* The importance of food; Chief dietary faults; Construction of a rational diet; The 'no-breakfast' plan; The question of dessert; Contamination by aluminium.

LECITHIN
THE FAT FIGHTER

Paul Simons. *Today, in the United Kingdom, more than 400 people died from coronary heart disease. It was the same yesterday and it will be the same tomorrow.* One of the main causes of heart disease is too much cholesterol in the blood. This book is about a biological emulsifier called lecithin, which keeps fats (including cholesterol) in suspension, allowing them to pass through the artery walls, preventing the build-up of hard deposits. Lecithin, 'miracle' product of the soya bean, also improves the nervous system, protects the liver and kidneys from disease and is an invaluable aid to slimmers!

MODERN HERBALISM FOR DIGESTIVE DISORDERS
AN ENCYCLOPAEDIA OF NATURAL HEALING

Frank Roberts M.N.I.M.H. Many years in the making, this book gives causes, symptoms, signs and curative prescriptions for digestive ills, including acidosis, alkalosis, appendicitis, constipation, diarrhoea, duodenal ulcer, gall stones, gastric ulcer, liver disorders and stomach troubles. Manner of presentation enables readers to find their ailments quickly and discover their exact treatment and prescription. An outstanding feature is a method whereby suspected diseases can be identified in their early stages. This is a truly comprehensive reference manual to modern practical herbalism for all digestive diseases.

THE REAL FOOD COOKBOOK
WHOLEFOOD DISHES FOR HEALTHY NUTRITION

Vivien & Clifford Quick. Wholefood cooking is fun—and healthy! This wonderful cookbook includes a feast of appetizing meals, party recipes, gourmet menus—everything your body needs, except junk foods! The authors introduce nutritional science into the kitchen, with astonishing results. Most dietitians know little about culinary art, and few cooks plan meals from the nutritional viewpoint. The Quicks bridge this gap triumphantly and this book is the result. It proves that wholesomeness does not lie in stodgy, over-cooked food. Eat by these rules and never again will your stomach quarrel with your palate!

SELENIUM
THE ESSENTIAL TRACE ELEMENT YOU MIGHT NOT BE GETTING ENOUGH OF

Alan Lewis. Here are the facts about this essential mineral — one of the most vital of the twenty or so trace elements that the body needs — but, because Britain is a low-selenium area, most of us don't get enough of it. This book reveals the link between low-selenium levels and the incidence of ill-health. It includes exciting new material on the use of selenium in the treatment of rheumatism and arthritis, and shows how it is beneficial in the treatment of heart disease and cancer. Explores its remarkable potential and gives vital information on the role of selenium in a balanced and healthy diet.